Contents

Getting Started	1
Tips for Using the Question Guide	3
Comprehension Strategies	5
Title page	7
Page One	9
Page Three	11
Page Four	13
Page Six	15
Page Eight	17
Page Nine	19
Page Ten	21
Page Eleven	23
Page Twelve	25
Page Thirteen	27
Page Fourteen	29
Page Fifteen	31
Page Sixteen	33
Page Seventeen	35
Page Eighteen	37
Page Nineteen	39
Page Twenty-one	41
Page Twenty-two	43
Words and Phrases Used in Chronological Order	45

TANYA POPOVSKI

The Pretend Friend

Question Guide

Published by PoP-O Books 2019

Copyright © 2019 Tanya Popovski

www.popobooks.com.au

Copying of this book for educational purposes: All rights reserved. No part of this publication may be reproduced, stored in a retrieval system, or transmitted in any form or by any means, electronic, mechanical, photocopying, recording or otherwise, without the prior written permission from the publisher.

A catalogue record for this book is available from
the National Library of Australia.

Book cover design and formatting services by Self-publishingLab.com

First edition 2019

ISBN 978-0-6484160-8-1

Getting Started

Kindergarten and year-1 reading expectations are quite different to those of mid to upper primary. In the early years, the focus is on decoding (learning how to read using symbols, sounds, sentences, and visual features). As the reader moves through the grades, the focus of reading in the classroom is about making meaning. The reader is then taught skills to deepen their understanding in order to read to learn.

The chosen book should be at a level below the reader's reading level. If you judge that the text is too difficult for the reader, choose a book at a lower level. This will allow the reader to concentrate on the meaning of the story, thereby encouraging higher-order thinking.

There is no need for pre-reading since a competent reader at this level will be able to read the text. The book should not be read in one sitting. Ask the comprehension questions after the reader has finished the text on each page. Continue to do this for approximately fifteen to twenty minutes. It is acceptable to take more than two sessions to complete questioning of the story. Go at the pace of the reader.

Tips for Using the Question Guide

The symbol ✪ indicates that an explanation for the word or phrase used can be found in the list at the back of this guide, which you can refer to for further clarification.

This book should not be seen as a text but rather a conversation of learning. When you have asked the reader each comprehension question, give them time to think before responding. The answers have been provided so you can give the reader the answer, which becomes a teachable moment.✪

If the reader has limited experience with a particular concept, take the opportunity to explore it further through the use of other resources (books, internet, etc). To use **Stop Annoying Me** as an example, if the reader has no understanding of the way a bull behaves, the words 'raging bull' will have no meaning. In this instance, you could take a moment to explain.

The answers provided in the **Question Guide** are general, and are given as examples only of acceptable answers. If the reader's answer is not relevant to the text, or cannot be justified with evidence from the text, this becomes a teachable moment. Give the answer, and show how you worked it out. The reader's responses do not have to cover all of the suggested answers.

If the reader's prediction of the title is not relevant to the clues on the page, avoid correcting their prediction straightaway. Instead, wait until they have finished reading the story to address the initial prediction. For example, you could say: 'At the beginning of the story, you predicted that the title would be [*repeat the reader's initial prediction*]. Now that you've read the story, how accurate do you think your prediction was? What clues could you have used on the title page to help you predict more accurately?'

The superscript numbers at the end of the questions relate to the tracking sheets (purchased separately at www.popobooks.com.au) and are linked to the Australian Curriculum.

Comprehension Strategies

Good learners draw on a range of comprehension strategies to deepen their understanding of written text. The *Question Guide* has been intentionally formulated to use the six comprehension strategies to explicitly teach how we understand texts. They are colour coded, with each colour corresponding to one of the six strategies.

Making connections Learners make connections with self, text and what is happening in the world.

Predicting Good readers use the information from illustrations, text and experiences to predict what will be read.

Questioning Good readers clarify meaning and aim for a deeper level of understanding by posing and answering questions.

Monitoring Good readers know what to do if something in the text doesn't make sense.

Visualising Good readers bring text to life by creating mental pictures from what they are reading.

Summarising Good readers are able to locate the most important ideas in a text and retell them in their own words.

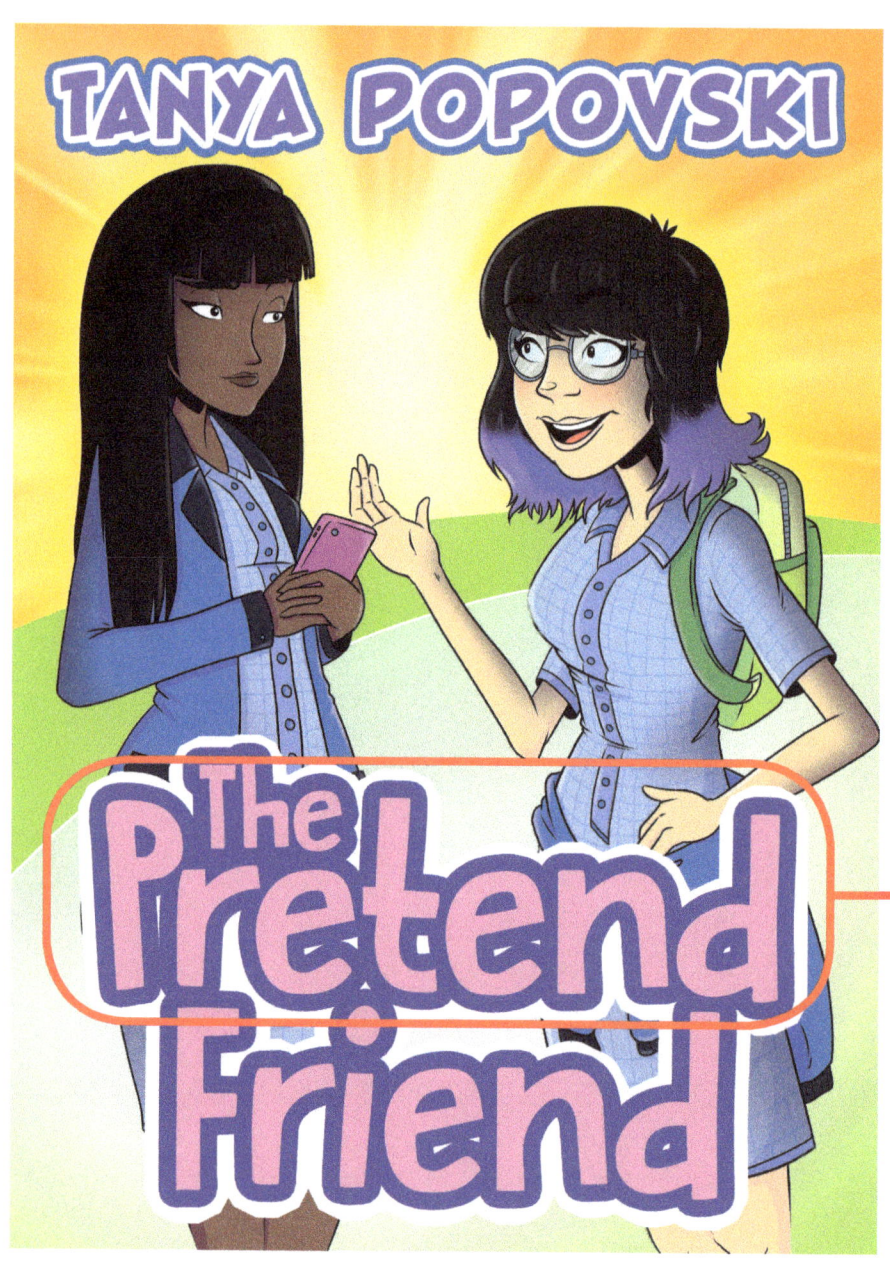

Title page

Allow the reader to read the title and look at the illustration.

Looking at the tile and the illustration on the front cover, what do you predict the story is about?[1]
Reader to respond based on the information on the front cover.

 What does the adjective ✪ 'pretend' mean?[2]
Pretend: to act in a false way in order to trick, to imagine or make believe

What is a friend?[17]
Friend: a person whom you know well and like, and who knows and likes you

What qualities do you look for in a friend?
trustworthiness
reliability
honesty
dependability
supportiveness

What does the illustration tell you about the characters?[10]
There are two girls.
Possibly they are friends.
They seem to be teenagers.
They are still going to school because they're wearing backpacks and uniforms.

Mikayla and Bella had been the best of friends since kindergarten. They knew each other so well because they had spent nearly every moment together. They knew silly little things about each other, all the things that didn't really matter to anyone but them.

Bella knew which teddy bear Mikayla loved to hug when she was feeling worried.

Mikayla knew that Bella liked her lunch to be in the glittery lunchbox rather than the yellow one.

As they grew up together, their likes and dislikes were very similar.

Page One

Allow the reader to read the text.

When did Mikayla and Bella become friends?[8]
In kindergarten

Do you have a friend you have known for a long time?
Various responses

If yes, name two things about you both that are similar.[3]
Various responses

Name two things about you both that are different.[3]
Various responses

Have a look at the table. What information does it give you?[4]
Mikayla and Bella like fashion, lip-gloss and reading, and neither likes vegetables or scary movies.

How does this table support the text you have just read?[5]
It shows specific things that Mikayla and Bella like and dislike. It shows how similar they are to one another.

Why do you think there are crosses and hearts on the table?[6]
The table has been written by one of the girls. The crosses indicate dislikes and the hearts indicate likes.

Page Three

Allow the reader to study the illustration.

What information does this illustration give the reader?[10]
The text states that Mikayla and Bella have been friends since they were little. We can infer ⭐ that the illustration shows them when they were in kindergarten because they look younger and are in a classroom.

Mikayla and Bella helped each other in class, and always looked out for one another.

Mikayla was good at spelling, and Bella was good with numbers. When Bella was trying to solve a maths problem, during sharing time she would ask Mikayla to help her.

When Bella was writing a story, she would ask Mikayla to edit her work and point out her spelling errors. This made it easier for Bella to make sure her work was correct before she published it.

They were a good team, and they used each other's strengths well. They were so close, their parents joked that they were joined at the hip.

Page Four

What are the main ideas⭐ so far?[27]
Mikayla and Bella are very good friends.
They are very similar in what they like and dislike.
They use each other's strengths to help each other.

What does it mean that they 'always looked out for one another'?[2]
They took care of each other.

What is a hyperbole⭐?
Hyperbole is the use of figurative⭐ language, where exaggeration is used for emphasis or humour.

Are there any examples of a hyperbole⭐ you have heard before?
If the reader is unsure, share some of the examples listed in the glossary.

Can you pick out the hyperbole⭐ (exaggeration) in the text?[7]
'They were joined at the hip.'

What is this figurative⭐ language emphasising?[9]
The two girls were always together.

During lunch and recess they were always inseparable. They played together, whispered secrets to each other, and relied on each other at all times. Even when they weren't together, they used social media to stay in touch. They sent each other messages and posted photos to record every aspect of their lives.

Their days in primary school went without a hitch, and they both had fond memories of this time. Scarlett, Emma, Matilda and Lily were part of their friendship circle, but everyone knew that Mikayla and Bella were the very best of friends and no one came between them.

Page Six

Allow the reader to read the text.

Are there any words that you are unsure of?
If the reader says no, ask the following:

What does the word 'inseparable' mean? Use the context ✪ to try and work out its meaning.²
Inseparable: impossible or difficult to divide, tending to remain together

What is meant by the term 'social media'?¹⁷
Websites and applications that allow users to share their lives through social networking
Social: in the company of others

Which forms of social media have you heard about before?¹¹
Snapchat: users share videos and pictures that self-destruct after a few seconds
Instagram: users share their lives with friends through photos
Facebook: a networking site where users share profiles, videos, photos, news and messages to keep in touch with others

Do you use any form of social media? If so, for what purpose?¹¹
Reader to give a personal response

What do the words 'went without a hitch' mean? Use the context ✪ to try and work out the meaning.²
The girls' lives were without any problems up until that point.

What evidence in the text supports the fact that the girls were the very best of friends?⁸
The text states that they played together, whispered secrets to each other, and relied on each other at all times. They spent time with other friends, but they all knew that 'no one got in their way'. They were inseparable.

The author has spent a lot of time describing how close the two girls were and had been for a long time. Why do you think this is important?¹²
The writer wants the reader to understand how connected the girls were as friends.

When they started high school, the first sign of trouble appeared between the best friends.

Bella seemed different to Mikayla. She didn't rely on Mikayla as much as she used to. Mikayla would often hear Bella whispering to her new friends, and she didn't include Mikayla as much as she used to.

Mikayla began to feel a little left out, but her parents tried to reassure her.

'It's all part of growing up and meeting new people,' her dad said.

'That's right,' said her mum, 'branching out and meeting new people is natural.'

Her parents encouraged her to do the same. Mikayla kept reminding herself that Bella would always be her best friend.

Page Eight

Allow the reader to read the text.

How would you have felt if you were Mikayla?[13]
Upset, disappointed, hurt, confused

When Mikayla's parents 'encouraged her to do the same', what were they referring to?[15]
Meeting new people

What do you think was really happening here?[14]
The friends were growing apart.
Mikayla was too reliant on Bella.

What did you have to do to make these inferences⭐?[18]
To make inferences it is important to look at the clues in the text. Previously the girls were very close ('inseparable'), but now Mikayla was feeling left out because Bella was forming friendships with others.

Page Nine

Allow the reader to study the illustration.

Judging from Mikayla's expression, did she seem worried about Bella telling secrets?[10]
No, she was happily talking to her other friends.

Why do you think Mikayla didn't seem annoyed or angry?[20]
Mikayla trusted Bella and respected the fact that her friend could share secrets with other people.

Do you think Bella was being respectful to the other people at the table?[21]
No, she should have been speaking to everyone and not whispering secrets. If she wanted to have a private conversation, she could have done that away from the rest of the group.

How do you feel about secrets?[21]
Various responses

This is a good opportunity to talk about safe and unsafe secrets. Some secrets, such as birthday-party surprises and gifts, are safe. Some secrets are unsafe, such as keeping it a secret if someone touches you. Unsafe secrets can also include games that may be harmful to the players, or anything that makes you feel uncomfortable.

Mikayla was a bit of a procrastinator when it came to homework. When she was meant to be working she would often allow herself to become distracted by other things.

One day she went online to check one of her social-media pages and saw a post that was very distressing to her. She immediately felt uncomfortable and angry to think that someone was so nasty as to post a negative comment about her.

Who would do a thing like that?

She was tempted to respond to the post, but then she remembered what their teachers had told them about not responding to negative online posts. She followed their advice and decided to ignore the problem, hoping it would go away.

She decided not to tell her parents.

Page Ten

Allow the reader to read the text.

➡ What does the word 'procrastinator' mean? Use the context ⭐ to try and work out its meaning.²
Procrastinator: someone who puts things off

Could this situation be classified as bullying?
Yes, it could.

➡ What effect did this post have on Mikayla?⁸
She felt uncomfortable, distressed and angry.

➡ What adjectives ⭐ are used to tell us that this post was not a good thing?⁷
Nasty, negative

➡ What action did Mikayla decide to take?⁸
She ignored it
She didn't tell her parents

What do you think of Mikayla's course of action?²¹
Personal response

Page Eleven

Allow the reader to study the illustration.

Why is different about this illustration?[10]
The illustration is no longer in colour like the other pages; it is in black and white.

Why do you think the illustrator has created the illustration in black and white?[23]
Mikayla's mood had changed. The story was not as bright and happy as it had been; it was now dark, sad and full of despair.

At school the next day, Mikayla waited for the opportunity to be alone with Bella so she could share something that she didn't want anybody else to know about.

'Last night I read a horrible comment about me on social media,' she explained to Bella. The distress in her voice was obvious, but Bella didn't seem too concerned.

'Maybe it was just a joke,' Bella said, 'don't be too worried about it. I wonder who it could be.'

Mikayla felt a little relieved, knowing that her best friend didn't think the post was too serious. She trusted Bella, and decided to take her advice.

But every day there was another ugly post saying something derogatory about her. Mikayla began to feel unhappy that someone thought so badly of her that they would write such mean things.

Page Twelve

Allow the reader to read the text.

➡ From Bella's response, how do you think she felt about Mikayla's distress?[6]
She wasn't too concerned and told Mikayla not to worry.

➡ How did Mikayla feel about Bella's advice?[8]
Mikayla felt relieved that Bella thought it wasn't too serious.

➡ Why would Bella's attitude towards the situation make Mikayla feel better?[6]
Mikayla trusted her friend's advice.

What is your opinion of Bella's advice?
Personal response

➡ What is the meaning of the word 'derogatory'? Use the context ✪ to try and work out its meaning.[2]
Derogatory: displaying a critical or disrespectful attitude

➡ How does the language used enhance the feeling of sadness?[9]
The adjectives ✪ used in the text describe the same type of feeling: ugly, unhappy, mean, derogatory.

If you could be a friend to Mikayla, what advice would you give her?
Various responses

Suggestions:
Tell an adult
Report the bullying
Remove the social media

26

Mikayla's personality began to change. Instead of being a happy, bubbly and outgoing person, she became someone who didn't want to hang out with friends anymore. Her room became her safe haven.

Page Thirteen

Allow the reader to read the text.

Mikayla's personality changed. How does the text describe this change?[8] Previously she was a happy, bubbly and an outgoing person, and she became someone who didn't want to go out with her friends and didn't want to leave her room.

Mikayla was disappointed that Bella didn't seem to notice how distraught she was. She often found herself looking at her classmates suspiciously, wondering who was doing this to her.

Page Fourteen

Allow the reader to read the text.

What does the word 'distraught' mean? Use the context ✪ to try and work out its meaning.[2]
Distraught: anxiously worried

From the information in the illustration, what can you infer about Bella's reaction to Mikayla's distress?[10]
Bella wasn't all that interested or concerned because she was looking at her phone while Mikayla was talking to her.

Mikayla cried a great deal and tried to keep all of the horror to herself. She worried that if anybody knew about the terrible things that were being said about her, they would start to believe them. Even Mikayla was starting to believe them herself.

As soon as she got home each day, she would run straight to her room, shut the door and check to see if there was a new post on social media. She was so upset by what was happening that she felt like she would break into a thousand pieces.

Page Fifteen

Allow the reader to read the text.

What was concerning about Mikayla's behaviour?¹⁰
She was upset all the time.
She didn't share her problems with someone she trusted.
She was focusing on Facebook.

Why was this concerning?⁶
Mikayla never used to be stressed and sad like this.

What could happen if Mikayla continued with this behaviour?¹³
Mikayla could become sick, both physically and mentally.

What is the main reason for this illustration?²³
To show how upset Mikayla was.

What word would describe Mikayla at this point?¹⁷
Various responses
Suggestions: victim, lonely, desperate, depressed, lost

Which statement in this sentence is a hyperbole ⭐ (exaggeration)?⁷
'She was so upset by it all that she thought she would break into a thousand pieces.'

One afternoon, Mikayla's parents sat her down and asked her how she was feeling.

'We've noticed a change in you,' her mum said, 'and we're very concerned.'

Mikayla began to cry. When she told her parents exactly what had been going on, they looked at each other in disbelief.

'Show us exactly what's been posted,' her dad said.

Mikayla had kept screenshots of all the posts because she realised it might be important to keep the evidence.

'We want you to deactivate your social-media account immediately,' her mum said. 'That way the bully won't be able to use this platform anymore.'

'It's important not to be silent about bullying,' her dad said. 'You've done the right thing by not

Page Sixteen

Allow the reader to read the text.

Skim and scan ⭐ the text to see if there any words that you are unsure about.
If the reader does not offer up any words, ask the following:

➡ What is the definition of the word 'deactivate'?[17]
Deactivate: to make inactivate, to not be operational

➡ What is the definition of the word 'platform'?[17]
Platform: web-based technology that enables social media services and solutions

➡ What is an antonym ⭐ of the word 'disbelief'?[19]
Belief, acceptance

What is a bully?[17]
A person who is cruel, insulting or threatening to others who are weaker, smaller or in some way vulnerable

➡ Why did Mikayla's parents ask her how she was feeling?[6]
They had noticed a change in her behaviour and were worried about her.

➡ According to the text, why was it a good thing to deactivate the social media account?[8]
The bully would no longer be able to post anything on Facebook. The platform is the technology that enables different forms of social media.

What is the main idea?[27]
Not to be silent about bullying

➡ Identify the right things that Mikayla did in dealing with the bullying.[8]
Admitting everything to her parents
Keeping evidence of the bullying
Taking screenshots of all the bully's posts

responding to the posts, because the bully wants you to respond. Keeping the evidence of the posts was also good thinking.'

Her parents explained that cyber bullying was a serious crime, and if they couldn't find out who was doing it they would take the evidence to the police.

Mikayla's dad conducted a little investigation of his own, and what he discovered shocked the entire family.

Page Seventeen

Allow the reader to read the text.

What do you think the huge shock was?[1]
Various responses

Mikayla's dad discovered that her **supposedly** best friend, Bella, was the one who had sent the messages.

Mikayla was hurt and angry. Questions rattled around in her head.

Why would Bella do such a thing to me?

Why would she want to hurt me so much?

Thinking back, Mikayla realised that she had seen a change in their friendship. They definitely weren't as close anymore. She remembered being annoyed that Bella hadn't comforted her or helped her when Mikayla told her about the social-media posts, the way she would have if it had happened to Bella.

It all made sense now. Mikayla decided that she would confront her so-called best friend. As she thought about how to do this, she felt as though a fire was raging inside her.

Page Eighteen

Allow the reader to read the text.

Why is the word 'supposedly' in bold text?[16]
Because Bella was supposed to be Mikayla's best friend, but instead she was the bully

What is the definition of the word 'confront'?[17]
Confront: to stand up to boldly

What are the pros and cons of Mikayla's decision to confront Bella?[24]
Pros: – By asking Bella about the problem directly, Mikayla found it easier to deal with it.
– Mikayla had the opportunity to stand up to the bully and let her know how it had affected her.
Cons: – If the confrontation had not been handled correctly it could have turned into a physical fight.
– Mikayla needed to have proof or Bella could have denied the accusation.

What would you do if you were in Mikayla's shoes?
Various responses

Can you identify the metaphor ⭐ in the text?[7]
'A fire raging inside of her'
If the reader does not know what a metaphor is, refer to the explanation in the back of the book to teach this concept.

Why has the author used this metaphor ⭐?[9]
The metaphor gives the reader a clear understanding of how Mikayla was feeling. Metaphors are used to make writing more interesting.

How can you visualise the outcome of the confrontation?[24]
Various responses

In a safe environment, Mikayla told Bella that she knew that she was the one who'd been posting all the nasty comments.

Bella looked at Mikayla with a smirk on her face. Her only reply was, 'It was just a joke. Don't take it so seriously.'

Mikayla couldn't believe what she was hearing. 'A joke?' she said. 'Well, I didn't find it funny, and isn't that what a joke should be? You knew what I was going through. I confided in you and you pretended to be my friend. Don't ever speak to me again. You're not a good friend, and I feel sorry for anyone who thinks you are.'

Mikayla walked away from Bella with her head held high. She felt relieved that she'd been able to say what she'd wanted to say, but she also felt sad.

Page Nineteen

Allow the reader to read the text.

➤ Why did Mikayla take Bella seriously even though Bella said it was just a joke?[22]
A joke is not meant to hurt someone.
A joke is meant to encourage laughter for all involved.

➤ What inference ✪ can you make about Mikayla's feelings by the words 'walked away with her head held high'?[2]
She was proud that she had confronted her bully.

➤ Should Mikayla have remained friends with Bella simply because they had been friends for a very long time?[21]
No, a friend is not worth keeping if they are bullying you.

➤ What effect do you think this confrontation had on Bella?[13]
She didn't seem too affected because she had a 'smirk on her face' when Mikayla told Bella that she knew. Bella didn't attempt to apologise or show regret for what she had done.

Page Twenty-one

Allow the reader to study the illustration.

What made this environment a safe one?[10]

This environment was safe because there was a teacher in the classroom. The teacher would have been able to calm the situation down if it had become heated.

After Mikayla's brave stand, it took her a little while to get back to her usual self, but in time she could laugh again and have a good time with her new friends.

She became very cautious about who she accepted as a friend. She knew it was better not to have Bella in her life than let her bully and torment her. As bad as the situation had been, she had learned valuable lessons.

Mikayla eventually started using social media again, but only occasionally. She had much more fun doing things with her family and friends, and not spending so much time on social media.

Page Twenty-two

Allow the reader to read the text.

➡️ The text refers to Mikayla's 'brave stand'. What does this mean?[2]
She confronted Bella and stopped being her friend.

➡️ Why would Mikayla be 'cautious' about friends?[18]
She had had a bad experience with someone she had known for a long time.

Retell ⭐ the story.[25]
Mikayla and Bella were best friends in primary school.
The relationship changed in high school, but Mikayla still thought they were friends.
Mikayla was bullied online.
Mikayla became sick and withdrew from life because of the bullying.
Her parents took action.
Mikayla confronted Bella.
Mikayla started to enjoy life again.

What valuable lessons did Mikayla refer to?[27]
How to deal with bullying
Talking to someone about bullying
Standing up to a bully even if they are a friend

What would you do if you were ever bullied online?[20]
Talk to someone you trust
Shut down your social media account
Report the bullying

➡️ What main idea ⭐ does the story end with?[27]
Doing things with friends and family can be better than spending too much time on social media.

What generalisations ⭐ (general ideas) can you make about the story?[26]
Cyber-bullying is a serious offence.
It is important to report any form of bullying.

Words and Phrases Used in Chronological Order

teachable moment An unplanned opportunity that arises in the classroom where the teacher has an ideal chance to offer insight to their students; not something that can be planned for; a fleeting opportunity that must be sensed and seized by the teacher. If the reader is unable to answer the question, answers the question incorrectly, or after prompting is still unsure, take the opportunity to tell them the answer and show them how you reached that conclusion.

retell To determine what is important; to retell a story in sequence, and with the correct facts.

adjective A word that describes a noun (e.g. *a beautiful boy*, *a majestic swan*).

infer Using clues from the story to figure out something that the author doesn't tell you. Using facts, observations and reasoning to come up with an assumption or conclusion (e.g. ***The ground was wet and the leaves were moving around***. Inference: It had been raining and it was windy.) ***On Jocelyn's return from her holiday, her plants were limp and droopy***. Inference: Her plants had not been watered during the time that she was away.)

main idea/s Teaching readers to know what the main ideas are can be difficult. The main idea is the most important part of the story. It helps readers to understand what the story is mainly about without too much detail. Think of **who** and **what** to generate the main ideas.

hyperbole A figurative-language technique where exaggeration is used for emphasis or humour (e.g. *I am so hungry I could eat a horse. This car goes faster than the speed of light. I had a ton of chores to do. My mum is going to kill me*).

figurative A meaning that is different from the basic meaning; expressing an idea in an interesting way by using language that describes something else (e.g. *It's raining cats and dogs*. This is a figurative description of heavy rain; if the meaning were literal, cats and dogs would be falling from the sky).

context The words, sentences, and ideas that come before and after a word or phrase.

skim and scan To skim is to read text very quickly; to scan is to locate specific pieces of information in the text without having to read each individual word.

antonym A word that has an opposite meaning to another word.

metaphor A figure of speech in which a word or phrase is applied to an object or action to which it is not literally applicable (e.g. *The hospital was a freezer. The classroom is a zoo*).

generalisation/s A broad statement that applies to many examples, formed from several examples or facts in a story. Find the most important ideas in the story and justify (prove) your answer.

inferential Drawing conclusions on the basis of evidence and reasoning.

Learn with

www.ingramcontent.com/pod-product-compliance
Lightning Source LLC
Chambersburg PA
CBHW040555010526
44110CB00054B/2722